The Early Church Today Series

THE LIFE OF ABBA JOHN KAME

THE EARLY CHURCH TODAY SERIES

Volume 5

The early leaders of the Church, tasked with shepherding Christ's flock, left us spiritual wealth that is too often neglected in modern times. The Early Church Today Series, published by the St. Mary & St. Moses Abbey Press, aims to help make that richness more accessible to readers, inviting them to see the applicability of the early Church to our walk with God today. By sharing practical selections from the writings of the early Church, aided by meaningful editorial supplements and revisions, each book will attempt to diminish impediments and bring to light what the Church has to offer.

THE LIFE OF
ABBA JOHN KAME

Revision of the Coptic Life and Translation of
the Arabic Life by

St. Mary and St. Moses Abbey

Translation of the Coptic Life by

M.H. Davis

The Life of Abba John Kame

Translation of the Arabic Life by St. Mary & St. Moses Abbey.

Translation of the Coptic Life by M.H. Davis.

Copyright © 2024 Coptic Orthodox Diocese of the Southern U.S.A.

All rights reserved.

Designed & Published by:
St. Mary & St. Moses Abbey Press
101 S Vista Dr, Sandia, TX 78383
stmabbeypress.com

All Scripture quotations in the footnotes of this book, unless otherwise indicated, are taken from the New King James Version® Copyright © 1982 by Thomas Nelson, Inc. Used by permission. All rights reserved.

Cover Icon: Wall icon of Abba John Kame, housed in St. Mary and St. Moses Abbey.

CONTENTS

The Life of Abba John Kame   7

Appendix A:
The History of the Relics of Abba John Kame   46

Appendix B:
The Monastery of Abba Teroti   48

About the Text   51

Bibliography   52

✠

THE LIFE OF ABBA JOHN KAME

A portion from the life and the discipline of our blessed and Spirit-endued father and God-clad, cross-bearing, revered priest, Abba John Kame, for a profit unto every one who shall hear it. And moreover the day whereon he went to rest was the 25th of the month Koiahk.[1] In the peace of God. Amen.

His Upbringing

Well indeed has our good Savior already said in the holy gospel, "You are the light of the world. A city cannot be hid that is set on a hill. Neither do (men) light a lamp and put it under a bushel; rather they set it on the candlestick, that it may give light unto all that are in the house. Let your light so shine before men, that they may see your good works and glorify your father which is in heaven." In very deed the light of our blessed father, Abba John Kame has attained unto the gates of heaven and the sweet

---

1   Koiahk, Tubah, and Hathor are Coptic months.

savor of his virtues has reached unto the throne of God and the angels and all the saints have rejoiced at his honor. The life of our blessed father gave forth shining splendor, even as the shining rays of the sun, giving light unto the uttermost ends of the earth. The sweet savor of his virginity has spread abroad as the sweet smell of the rose in the month Pharmouthi. He was choicer than spices, he was a holy gift unto the Lord, of more value than pearls and precious stones. The Lord sanctified him from (the time) when he was in the womb. His name has won renown in all the world, and has become a sweet-smelling ointment in all the churches. For this cause has my soul loved him, and therefore I desire, O my beloved, to set moving the instrument of my feeble tongue, that I may tell some few things from the Life of our blessed and holy father, John Kame. When I consider his lofty good deeds, I am afraid and tremble, more especially when I know the poverty of my understanding and the weakness of my tongue. But the prayers of our holy father raise up my feebleness, he that is in our midst today, rejoicing with us on the day of his feast, encouraging us that we may tell particularly his holy Life. Then hear me with attention, O my beloved, you God-loving people, for I would bid you today to a kingly feast, I would set before you a kingly table and a spiritual, that I might feed you with a heavenly food, which is the Life that is full of encouragement of our father. Seeing that I am not myself fitted to do

The Life of Abba John Kame

this, but rather I liken myself unto the poor widow, that did cast two mites into the treasury, therefore will I betake myself unto the preface and will tell clearly that which the Holy Spirit shall furnish unto us through the prayers of our holy and all-saintly father, Abba John Kame, according as our fathers have told us.

Now this holy man of whom we tell was of a village which is called Jepromonnonson, in the name of Sais, and he gave himself unto virtue from his childhood. He was sweet in his nature and unto all men mild, zealous in virtue and prudent in his words, sober in his judgment, pure in his body, sanctified in his soul, good toward all men, a lover of charity, a lover of strangers, righteous in his soul, wise and of understanding, righteous in all his ways, devout in the faith, going early to the church of Christ, fasting at all times, praying continually, meditating the name of our Lord Jesus Christ with great fervor by day and by night, keeping his body in subjection, making it the servant of his soul, withdrawing himself from all worldly cares and from thought of the matter, and ease of this life and from the deceit of the flesh, bringing to naught his sin-loving [...][2], forgetting the things of this life for they swiftly pass away, and eager for the age of light and the inheritance of the righteous. He was adorned with all good things by the gift of the Holy Spirit; in a word, he served the Lord with all his

---

2   Missing word here in the Coptic text.

might, keeping the commandments of our God-clad father Abba John.

His Marriage

It is told us concerning him that while he was yet a youth and continuing in these good works that we have recorded and more than these, he was betrothed unto a maiden, a virgin, that he should take her to wife, according to the laws of nature. And when they had made the marriage feast for him and her, as was befitting, they set him with her within the bride-chamber and they closed the door. But the righteous man, our holy father, spread forth his hands and prayed unto the Lord, desiring him to give him strength in that which he had it in mind to fulfil. And he said, "'Lord God of hosts I was cast upon You since I was in the womb, You are my God since I was in the belly of my mother.' Grant unto me, my Lord, that I may be in the purity of virginity unto the end and grant unto your servant also, she that has been bidden with me, that she may be worthy of the lot of the five wise virgins. Glory be unto you for ever. Amen."

And his bride looked and saw the holy man standing and his hands spread forth and his ten fingers were as it were ten lamps of fire, and she was in fear and trembling. Then the righteous man called unto her and said mildly unto her: "Come near unto me, that I may speak with you, according to the love of Christ, for the salvation at once of your soul and of mine also, according as Christ has said in the holy Gospel: 'None has aught greater than this love, that one lay down his life for his friend.' Seeing that we are united one to another in a union after the flesh for the begetting of children in sorrow of heart yet if you will hearken unto me, we will unite together in a spiritual union for the begetting of virtues. For seeing that we have been united one with another in the cares of life, if you will hearken unto me, we will unite ourselves in an immaterial union. Let us depart far from the sweetness of the flesh which is for a time, that we may be set free in the day of the true judgement. If so be that we keep our virginity and our bodies pure, we shall ourselves be made together worthy of the inheritance of the righteous. For the man that has married a wife and the woman that has married a husband, have taken thought for the things of this life, that they might please one another; but they that have not married have taken thought for the things of the Lord, that they might please Him. It were good for us therefore that we should despise the things of the earth and seek after those of heaven, that we should renounce the things of a season and seek after those of eternity.

"Instead of the bride-chamber of this world, we should be made worthy of the bride-chamber that is in heaven. In exchange for the gladness and the perfume of our bridal state that shall pass away, we may be made worthy of the ointment of heaven and the oil of gladness, that which flows forth from the church of the first-born. In exchange for the children that we should beget in the flesh, we shall become the children of God and the companions of his angels and shall rejoice with the five wise virgins, they that trimmed their lamps and went in unto the feast with the bridegroom. The earth shall swiftly pass away and the glory of it, gold shall perish and silver rust, the beauty of the body shall perish and shall be dissolved in the tomb, but 'he that does the will of God shall abide for ever.'"

Now when she heard these things, his blessed bride—for she was indeed blessed by reason of her good disposition—became filled with the joy of the Holy Spirit and she cast herself upon the ground and worshipped God. And she said, "Glory unto You, O Christ, that You have not deprived me of the aim of my soul's zeal. You have granted me the desire of my soul and of the prayer of my lips You have not deprived me. In exchange for suffering, You have given me rest, for sorrow of heart You have given me gladness, for bondage freedom, for things perishable things imperishable, for the things of the earth, the good things that are in heaven, in exchange for death You have given me life eternal. You have illuminated me, my Lord, by means of Your servant, him whom You have already chosen from (the time) that he was in his mother's belly, that he might call many in unto Your kingdom; for Yours is the glory for ever. Amen." Then she laid hold of the feet of our holy father and kissed them, saying after this manner, "Blessed be the hour wherein I met you and the day wherein you were born, O you holy one of God. Verily, O my beloved brother, you have loved me as your (own) soul, you have given unto me honor and have glorified me; you have given life unto my soul. So then, if you have set it in your heart, O my beloved brother, that you should keep your virginity, I likewise rejoice that I should keep mine also. For you, my beloved brother, are lord of my body, according to the saying of Paul the apostle, and are agreed that you should be a virgin, so I too am ready to obey you unto the day of my death. For seeing that your sweet words have made fat my bones and have entered in unto the senses of my soul, so have I also understood them aright with the understanding ears of my heart, those things concerning which our Lord Jesus Christ spoke in the holy gospel, saying, 'He that has ears to hear, let him hear.'" And when the blessed John heard these things from the blessed woman, he rejoiced the more and gave glory unto God. And they made a covenant together, they both, in the presence of the Lord, that they should keep their virginity according to the agreement of their heart.

Great indeed is your honor, O our holy father; your name is filled with perfume in heaven and upon the earth. Well has David said in his prophecy, speaking of your honor, "He that makes a solitary to dwell in a house." Verily was this saying fulfilled in these blessed ones. O, who shall tell of the great courage of our holy father and the purity of his heart, of the firmness of his reason and of his great continence and his wondrous uprightness. For at this time there is no man who shall be able thus to contain himself. Lo, I myself marvel that your thoughts have not troubled you, being in this same house with this woman. Who shall approach a fire and shall not be burnt, who is he that has walked like you upon coals of fire and has not known? Who has conquered pleasures as you did? For you have trampled on all the passions of the flesh, for you did become a temple of the Holy Spirit, according to the saying of the Lord: "The wind blows where it wishes;" that is to say you, O our all-saintly father. Therefore did you extinguish the flame of fornication, and of you also has the Lord said: "There be men that have made themselves eunuchs for the kingdom of heaven." Let them be ashamed now that defile their bodies with pollutions and with unnatural sins, when they hear concerning our holy father, that he had not intercourse with his wife.

The Miracle of the Vine

Now after these things a wondrous marvel came to pass. God commanded and caused a vine to spring up in the bride-chamber, laden with fruit and spreading forth in the whole house. And this happened for a faithful proof and for a testimony to the purity of

The Life of Abba John Kame

life of our most saintly, holy father, and of his lofty good deeds. When our holy father John and his wife saw this marvel, they were the more established in the love of Christ, giving thanks unto the Lord and glorifying him in praisings and in blessings, by day and by night, at all hours, being in great gladness and praising God, like the angels.

Heading for Scetis

And after all these things it came to pass in the night that he saw in a vision, while he stood in prayer, a man of light, and he spoke with him, saying, "Be not neglectful of this ministration unto which you are called through the Lord God. When you rise in the morning, go to Scetis, to the desert of our father Abba Macarius, and inquire after the dwelling of my father Teroti and become a monk with him and wear the habit of the angels, for that blessed old man is righteous and fitted for the salvation of many souls. For this is the will of the Lord." When he arose at dawn, our holy father called unto his bride and said unto her, "I bid you farewell, my good sister, for I am bidden of the Lord to depart and to become a monk. You also, O my beloved sister, do you apply yourself to the salvation of your soul. So I bid you farewell until we see one another in the kingdom of heaven." When she heard these things from the holy one, she was in great sorrow of heart, and said unto him, "I pray you, O my lord brother, that you would remember me in your prayers, that the Lord may order my whole life according as it pleases Him." And the holy one said unto her, "Be of good courage, the Lord shall not forsake you." And he saluted her and departed from her in peace and went to the high-road, the grace of God assisting him, until he came to the holy monastery [lit. place; Cop. ⲧⲟⲡⲟⲥ] of our divinely-speaking and most pious, holy father, Abba Macarius, the all-virtuous champion, the chief of monkhood, the measure of virtue, the staff of age, the completion of the priesthood, he that was found worthy of the blessedness of the promises, according to the interpretation of his name. And he inquired and was shown the dwelling of our holy cross-bearing father, my father Teroti. When he knocked at the door, after the custom of the monks, the porter opened unto him the door, and said unto him, "What do you desire, my son?" He said unto him, "If it be the will of God, I desire to become a monk." And the porter told the old man concerning him and he caused him to he brought in in gladness. For unto our holy father, Abba Teroti, it had been revealed of the Lord, He telling him of the coming unto him of our righteous father. And when he saw him, giving forth splendor by the grace of the Lord, he gave glory unto God and received him with great willingness. And he said unto him, "Why this haste that you have made (to come) unto us, O my son?" Our holy father made answer with humility, his face cast down, saying, "I came here, O my holy

The Life of Abba John Kame

father, that I might remain under the shadow of your prayers, and entreat the Lord because of my sins." Then our holy father, Abba Teroti, desired to test him and he said unto him, "It befits the monk that he be withdrawn from all things evil and straitened as to all comforts of this world, even unto his speech." The holy man John said unto him, "I trust in your prayers that your heart shall have satisfaction in me."

And thus he put upon him the holy habit, knowing that this thing was from God, and he gave him a place apart wherein he might be in quiet. And he visited him, imparting unto him the word of the Lord and the holy service of those that had become renowned in virtue and the canon of the holy Synaxis of the hours, that he should pray every hour, according to the commandment of our father, Abba Agathon, the stylite, and that he should contend with the evil spirits of wickedness and vile passions and bring them to nought by the strictness of continence. So our holy father, Abba John, received all the words of the old man with great submission, increasing in grace daily by the loftiness of his way of life and the laborious exercises that he performed (both) in secret and openly. And when the holy old man Teroti learnt of his virtues, he glorified God, and so commended him before all men.

Now after these things it happened one evening, while our all-saintly father John was standing at prayer, that he beheld an angel of the Lord, standing before him in glory. And he said unto him, "Peace be unto you, you servant of God. When you rise in the morning, come forth from this place and go unto the cell of the great light Abba John. Go toward the west, far removed from all dwellings and make there a dwelling and live therein. For these things says the Lord: 'I will give you an inheritance in that place, I will gather unto you many people and you shall lead them unto the angelic work, and you shall be to them a leader and the savior of their souls. And there shall be for you a holy community, and by your name it shall be called. Your name shall be renowned in all the world. The Lord shall give unto you a lot in these deserts, because you have walked in the footprints of those that are become famous on this mount, and that have become rulers for them that have dwelt in the wilderness, namely the great Abba Macarius and Abba John, Abba Pishoi, and Maximus and Dometius, and seeing that you have striven after their likeness, you shall be with them in the same resting place, in the kingdom of heaven.' And I will visit you, according to the commandment of the Lord and your name shall be called John Kame, that you may fulfill all the will of the Lord."

And when he had said these things unto him, the angel departed from him and appeared unto his spiritual father and related all these things unto him. But when morning came, our righteous father arose and went unto our holy father, Abba Teroti, and told him those things that had been said unto him. And his father said unto him, "Go and fulfill the will of the Lord; for the Lord shall do unto you all things of which the angel spoke unto you." Therefore our holy father John Kame besought his father that he would bless him, and the holy old man Abba Teroti blessed him, even as Isaac blessed Jacob, saying, "The Lord God shall bless you that you may fulfill His holy will. Amen." And when our holy and all-saintly father had received his father's blessing, he journeyed, rejoicing, until he came to the place concerning which the angel had told him and he made there a cave, shutting himself within it and singing this psalm, saying, "You have set my feet upon a rock and established my footsteps, You have put a new song in my mouth, and a blessing unto our God. Amen."

His Spiritual Struggles

O who shall tell the lofty virtues of this righteous man and the combats wherein he conquered, which, if one should hear them, he would tremble! It is said also concerning our holy father that he wearied himself in his exercises beyond many of our fathers because of his strictness, and they bear witness concerning him that he was exalted in his way of life, even as Elijah the Tishbite. Also, it is said of him that when he stood at prayer, he was accustomed to bending the knee with great effort without interruption, as though he formed a ring, until the sweat of his body flowed down upon his feet like water, as though one should bathe himself therein and wet his whole body. For he made many thousand prostrations, such that if one should write them, he would not be believed of them that are without faith, for whose sake the wrath of God comes. But why do I speak thus? For indeed you all bear witness with me to those things that I tell. In truth, O my beloved, I am as one in a great and boundless sea without means to reach the shore, because of the great virtues of our all-saintly father, John Kame. For indeed mine is a tongue of flesh and sinful lips; I am not able to tell of his honor. Yet when I see your eagerness and how gladly you desire to hear his Life, I myself take courage the more, my heart rejoices in gladness. Verily, O my beloved, you Christ-loving people, I am as sounding brass and a clanging cymbal, when I speak of the good deeds of our God-clad father, John, he whose Life and whose virtues may be likened unto those of the great Anthony, and especially all his acts, which shine as the stars of the morning, so that when I remember them I am at a loss and fearful and my mind is amazed. But I too shall say spiritually with the holy prophet David: "O Lord, open my lips and my mouth shall speak Your blessing."

It is told also concerning our all-saintly father, that many times he would not eat from Sabbath to Sabbath, but at other times he would not eat except every forty days. Many a time he would retire to the desert and be in quiet by himself, in austerities not to be described. Further they bear witness concerning him that he slept not, by day or by night, except only for a brief slumber, leaning against the wall, after which he would arise swiftly and would sing in this psalm, saying, "I will not give sleep to my eyes, nor slumber to my eye-lids, nor rest unto my temples, until I find a place for the Lord and a dwelling-place for the God of Jacob." And thereby his soul and his mind shone forth, and his face shone through the power of the Holy Spirit which rested within him, because of his purity; according as our Lord Jesus Christ, our good Savior, has said in the holy gospel: "He that hears My words and keeps them, he it is that loves Me; and he that loves Me My Father will love him and We will go unto him and make Our dwelling within him." It is told also concerning our holy father John, that all things that the brethren did, whether a (deed) of virtue or other matter, he would see them in secret. For this cause, therefore, was his name renowned everywhere.

The Appearance of the Virgin St. Mary

O who may tell the number of the manifestations and the mysteries and the revelations that he saw from time to time. For oftentimes he would see the glory of the Lord upon the altar as if it were a fire and would hear the angels singing the Trisagion at the time of the holy Anaphora. It is also told of our holy father John that oftentimes there appeared unto him the holy Mother of God, Mary, she who bore for us our Lord Jesus Christ, our true King, and she wished him peace and comforted him.

Now it happened in the holy night of the Lord's Day, while he stood performing his Synaxis, that the holy Mother of God, Mary, came in unto him in great and unspeakable glory and a multitude of angels accompanied her. He fell upon his face from fear, but the Mother of God raised him and said unto him, "Peace be unto you, John, beloved of my son Jesus, and of his good Father and of the Holy Spirit. Be of good courage and steadfast and become a mighty man, having great endurance, fighting against the evil hostile spirits, that contend with you. And lo, I am with you until you shall overcome them all and their evil and fulfill all the will of my Son. Further I will establish (my) covenant with you and will preserve my mercy for you; for I will abide in this place with you, because I love it; and it shall become for you a holy community, and there shall be unto you multitudes of children and they shall call it by your name; and shall build a church in your community and shall call it by my name; and the blessing of my Son and His peace and His protection shall abide in your community. The angels shall visit your monastery and shall watch over your children, that no traitor break through the walls of your dwelling-place for ever. As long as your children walk in your ways and do your bidding and keep your commandments and your laws and love one another in charity and remain in purity and righteousness, I will abide with them for ever and I will bless their ministration and their handiwork, and they shall inherit eternal life with you in the kingdom of heaven." And she gave unto him three gold *solidi*, having upon them the sign of the Cross and said unto him, "Take these and put them in the purse of the ministry (and) the blessing of my Son shall be in it for ever." (It is said, Behold, these lie in the monastery even unto this day). When she had said these things unto him, she wished him peace and filled him with strength, and she was hidden from him in great glory. But our righteous father was in great gladness by reason of the words the holy Mother of God, Mary, had said unto him and there came upon him a still greater power. And he sang saying, "I have sought after Your face O Lord, Your face O Lord, have I sought. Turn not Your face away from me, be unto me a helper, forsake me not, that I may fulfill Your will, O Lord my God, Amen."

It is told also regarding him that at the time when they were building the wall of the monastery and the towers, the angels of the Lord would help them in all their labors by the commandment of God; but especially the most high power of God was a fellow worker with them, through the mediation of the holy Mother of God, Mary. And the name of our holy father John became renowned in all places, so that everyone blessed him as a prophet and as a teacher in his generation, because he crucified his flesh, and his desires and his thoughts. He made all his cares the servants of our Lord Jesus Christ, our God, bringing forth the fruits of the Holy Spirit in love and gladness, and rejoicing and peace and long suffering and kindness, and goodness and faith and meekness and temperance. These things not only did he (himself) perform, but to everyone he taught that they should do them, saying unto them, "Whatsoever a man sows that shall he also reap. He that sows unto his flesh shall reap also of the flesh corruption, (but) he that sows unto the Spirit shall also of the Spirit reap eternal life." Verily, O our holy father, you have both sown and reaped spiritual fruit. Your fruits are increased unto you a hundred and sixty and thirty-fold.

His Wife Becomes a Nun

I desire, then, O my beloved, to relate unto you concerning the destiny of his blessed wife. Now it happened, when our holy father John departed from her and went into the desert, that she arose swiftly and distributed all she had to the poor and she shaved the hair of her head and became a nun. And she practiced many austerities and exercises in great number, so that her name was greatly renowned and there gathered unto her a multitude of virgins and they became nuns under her. And she built for them a nunnery and became a ruler over them. And she assisted them in good works and in the ways of the Lord, and thus became a leader for the salvation of many souls unto eternal life. And the virgins began to increase in number, the grace of God assisting them. And the blessed woman was the servant of the Lord and she increased in her days and went to rest at the Lord's pleasure, through the prayers of our holy father, Abba John. And lo, these others also our God-clad Father John brought in as gifts unto the Lord. Many indeed are the souls that you have saved from the evil devilish enemy, by your holy prayers.

Many Brethren Gather Around Him

What tongue of flesh or what heart of man shall tell of your uprightness and your glory in the measure of your honor, and of your constancy toward God. Even be it one whose heart is pure as are the angels and his mind like unto the incorporeal, yet shall he not be able to tell the fullness of your honor and the glory that the Lord has given unto you, in heaven and upon the earth; even as our Lord Jesus Christ has said in the holy gospel, "He that glorifies me, him will I glorify." For this cause I would indeed be silent, yet I fear lest I come under the charge of the wicked servant that hid in the ground the silver of his lord. Therefore will I be instant and prolong the discourse and will tell other few things from his upright deeds and the boundless victories of his austerities, such that should one tell them all, the discourse would be greatly extended. But we will leave aside many, choosing to tell some few, reminding you, O my beloved, that he became famous in the holy deserts and a teacher in his generation, even as Paul, that became the thirteenth of the apostles. Thus it was that our holy father, Abba John Kame, became the fifth in the holy places that were in Scetis, by the commandment of the Lord.

But after these things, while yet our holy father John dwelt in the cave, meditating[3] the saving name of our Lord Jesus Christ, our God, with prayers unceasing and secret petitions beyond telling—for no man knew the fullness of the sufferings that he endured, for he fled from the vain glory of men—it happened, when the evil demons saw his perfectness, they armed against him in troops and dark hosts, thinking to bring him down from the height of virtue and attacking his mind with evil thoughts unceasingly, by day and night and terrifying him with phantom forms. But the righteous man pursued after them all with the holy sign of the Cross. And when God saw his great endurance, he gave him rest from all thoughts.

And when many had heard concerning him and his virtues, a great multitude gathered about him, and they besought him that he would put upon them the habit of the monkhood. And there were (given) unto him many children and he formed them into

---

3   Or: reciting. Coptic, *meletan* (ⲙⲉⲗⲉⲧⲁⲛ). Arabic Life, *yatlo*.

a community, that they should build a dwelling-place. And they built a great ocean of dwellings and high towers and walls firmly established. And the brethren began to increase more and more and he taught them, for the salvation of their souls, that they should keep the unity of the right faith, and should love prayer and fasting, and love one another, and keep the purity of their body and soul, and that they should be lovers of the poor and lovers of charity, and should love solitude, and should put before them at all times the fear of the Lord. And he established for them canons and holy laws and set up for them a meeting-place, where they should meet together in the middle of the night and should sing psalmody and spiritual songs until the light dawn. And he bade them moreover one and all that they should pray each one apart. And by these (rules) and some others also which he delivered unto them, he caused them all to become fervent in godly zeal.

The Appearance of St. Athanasius the Apostolic

It is told also concerning our holy father that while yet he stood singing with the brethren by night, our father Abba Athanasius the apostolic appeared unto him and said unto him, "Peace be unto you, you good and faithful servant of God. Peace unto all your children and unto them that obey your laws. The sweet smell of your prayers has mounted up into the presence of God, as a remembrance for you for ever, and your name shall endure to all generations." And when our father Abba Athanasius had said these things unto him, he was hidden from him. Therefore was the holy man glad and he commanded his children that they should name the name of our father Abba Athanasius in the hymn of the Three Holy Children; and they do his bidding even unto this day, to the glory of God.

His Disciples

Now the first of his children he made of the order of disciples unto him, and these are their names: our father Shenouti the completion of the collecting together of this congregation; and my father Papa Mark, his successor after him, and my father Coluthus, and my father the deacon George, and my father Anthony, and my father George, of whom is born witness that they were worthy of the grace of the Holy Spirit. And if one should begin to tell the fullness of their good deeds, the discourse would increase greatly.

His Ordination as a Priest

And moreover after these things they laid hold of our holy father, and consecrated him priest against his will. When he was standing before the sanctuary and began the holy Anaphora, a glory of the Lord came upon the altar, as it were a fire. And when our holy father saw this sight, he glorified God.

Going South

And after these things our holy father was told by the angel that stayed by him that he should go unto the parts of Southern (Egypt), for the salvation of other multitudes of souls together, after the manner of our father Abba John and our father Abba Pishoi, the great lights. And our holy father called unto one of his children, namely our father Shenouti, his successor after him, and said unto him, "My son, I am called of the Lord to a ministry. Lo, I entrust to you the brethren, that you stand in this place and direct the brethren until I return unto you by the will of God." And by the grace of God he departed unto Southern (Egypt), the help of God guiding him, and he found a dwelling[4] and dwelt therein. O who can recount the austerities that he practiced there? And when the men of that place saw his virtues, there came multitudes unto him and became children unto him, and the name of that place[5] is called "Papa John Kame" even unto this day.

His Disciple Shenouti

But his disciple, being obedient unto his father, stood upon his feet all the days that our father passed in Southern (Egypt), standing in the place wherein our father left him when he departed from him,

---

4   Coptic: ⲧⲟⲡⲟⲥ. Arabic Life: a monastery.
5   Ibid.

showing endurance and directing the house, so that his body swelled like unto a pillar and the brethren besought him that he would sit a little and rest himself. (But) he consented not and the brethren set some stones about him, and he remained standing in great obedience; even as our holy father, Abba John Paké, when Apa Paphnouthius said unto him, "Wait for me that I may drink water," and forgot him, and departed unto the harvest and left Abba John standing, so that he passed the whole summer through; and he came and found him standing in the place where he had said unto him: "Wait for me." But when the Lord saw the faith of the disciple, he sent the angel and he took the hand of our holy father Abba John and brought him to Scetis, by the might of God. He told him concerning his disciple and he told him also, saying, "The day draws near wherein you shall have rest from all your labors and rightly take your rest with all the saints." Immediately the angel was hidden from him and the righteous man came to where the disciple was and said unto him, "Well done indeed, O my obedient son." And he touched his body, and it was made whole. And immediately he arose, and did a prostration [of reverence] to him, and his father blessed him. And when all the brethren knew, they gathered unto him and received blessing from him, for they loved him greatly, for he was to them both an encourager and a teacher for the salvation of their souls. And he performed many severe exercises in secret.

His Departure

And further, after these things, it pleased the king Christ to give him rest from all his labors and to translate him from this world, full of suffering and dangers and wretchedness, and to bring him again to the heavenly Jerusalem and the resting-places of light and the mansions on high and the tabernacles above, in exchange for his exercises and his austerities, and to give him eternal life in the land of the living. And the Lord visited him with a little fever and as he lay, he blessed the Lord. And all his children were gathered unto him, and they said unto him, "Our father, speak a word unto us." And he said unto them, "Do not hold disputations regarding heresies, neither go in to a house with women, nor put your trust in rulers, nor get for yourselves substance; (but) let your handiwork suffice you." And when he had said these things unto them, he lifted up his eyes and saw the companies that had come for him, clothed in glory, and a great company of angels and companies of the righteous that dwelt in the desert, after whose example he had striven. And being in the joy and the gladness of the Holy Spirit, he opened his mouth and yielded up his spirit into the hands of the Lord and his soul was taken up to heaven by the angels who had come for him. And he received of the Lord the heavenly prizes and the high rewards and he received the inheritance of all the saints.

His holy body was at once enshrouded with

great honor whilst it dispersed sweet odors like unto spices; and they bore him, singing before him, until they brought him unto the east of the church of our holy father, the hegumen, Abba John. And they made for him a vault beneath the ground and laid him therein; and over it they built a notable monument, and he was for a help unto everyone who prayed therein with faith. And the day wherein our holy and all-saintly father John went to rest was the 25th day of the month Koiahk. May (his) holy blessing be with us. Amen. And God poured out mercy upon his children and they began to increase and multiply and great blessing was on their ministration and great security and uprightness in their holy community, through the prayers of our holy father Abba John Kame and the mercy of God shall not cease to be with them for ever.[6]

Our father, St. Shenouti became his successor, the head over the brethren. Abba Shenouti was righteous, God-clad, capable of the word of teaching and the path of the Lord.

It is necessary for me to tell this marvelous story, which trusted witnesses made known to us, in honor of our father, St. Abba John Kame.

The Vision of the Syrian Anchorite

There was a Syrian elder, who was an anchorite,

---

[6] After this there are 8 folios missing in the Coptic Life. The missing section was supplemented and translated from the Arabic Life.

living in the land of Syria, established[7] in the anchoritic life, renowned throughout the East. He saw in a vision that as though he were caught up to the heavens and was made to stand before the throne of God. He saw thousands of thousands, and ten thousand times ten thousand of angels, praising God. Then he saw two monks, elders standing in great glory. When the elder saw them, he was astonished because of them, and he went to an angel and asked him, saying, "I beseech you, master, would you not tell me who these two monks are, who are clad in this glory and are standing in the midst of the angels?" He said to him, "The tall man is Abba Macarius, the father of the monks of the mountain of Scetis, and the other accompanying him is Abba John Kame who walked in his virtues."

When he rose up from the vision, he was greatly astonished at what he had seen. Then he said to himself, "I will rise and go to Egypt, and I will go up to the mountain of Scetis and worship in the monasteries of these righteous men." And he at once drew an icon of the two [men], according to the likeness which he saw, and he brought it with him to Egypt. So he came to the monastery of the great, the head of the monks, the saint, Abba Macarius, and prayed therein and prostrated before the holy bodies of the three Macarii. And from there he came to the cells of our father Abba John the hegumen and worshipped therein. After that he came to the holy

---

7   Literally: strong.

cenobium of our saintly father, Abba John Kame, and he prayed in their holy community.

The name of that Syrian elder was Marutha[8], for so his name was in Syriac. He related to the brethren what he had seen in his country and showed them the icon which he had drawn, and it is placed in his monastery to this day.

When he saw their works, their struggle, and their Psalmody, he remained with them to the day of his repose, and he left them his palm-leaf garment as an inheritance, which he put on at the time of his prayer, and through which he used to oppress his body.

The Establishment of a Church in the Monastery

And I will relate to you how they managed this holy fellowship and the pure church through the commands of God. In the days of our father St. Abba Macarius, the Archbishop of Alexandria,[9] he was stirred by God, like our father St. Abba Benjamin, to establish a church for them. For when he saw the multitude of the brethren, and that God had blessed them, so they were more than three hundred monks in number, some of whom were elders who would become wearied when they went up to the Great Church belonging to our father the God-clad,

---

8   Arabic: Maruta.
9   Abba Macarius I, the 59th Patriarch, AD 932–952.

The Life of Abba John Kame

Abba John the hegumen, to partake there of the Gift [lit. Corban], Archbishop Abba Macarius went up to the cells of our father Abba John the hegumen after the holy Feast of Theophany, accompanied by priests, and he went into the holy community of our father Abba John Kame. When he saw this fellowship [or cenobium], he was exceedingly glad, and he came to the place of the church which he had previously promised, and then consecrated it on the eighteenth of [the month of] Tubah after the name of St. Mary, and he ordained priests for them, to serve [in] this holy church. And this was by the command of the exalted God, like the consecration of the great church by our father Abba Benjamin among the cells of the monastery of Abba Macarius.

The Monasteries of Scetis

This church and this holy fellowship [or cenobium] belonging to our father Abba John Kame became the fifth in the ranking of the monasteries in Scetis, for the Lord has given beforehand two firm covenants. In the old covenant, through His prophets, Moses was the first, to whom the Lord delivered the law. And the Lord said to him that he should make four cities for refuge for the troubled souls. In truth the four monasteries in Scetis became a harbor of salvation for those persecuted by sins and the death caused by the devil. Then He said to him to make a dome [the tabernacle of meeting]. And make in the dome five courts, and make a sanctuary[10], and in the sanctuary make a table, and let there be five posts bearing the table, and five priests all serving in it. Let us understand and realize the words of the Books, and so we shall find the proof we are seeking concerning this holy fellowship [or cenobium] of our father Abba John Kame, because it became the fifth in all the monasteries according to the saying of the Lord God. For He spoke to Moses regarding the four cities, as a sign of the four monasteries: that is, the monastery of our father, the saint Abba Macarius, and our father Abba John [the Short], and our father Abba Pishoi, and our Roman fathers. Then He spoke concerning the five courts, that the holy fellowship [or cenobium] shall be given. I believe that these whom we have mentioned have become pillars and exceedingly luminous jewels in the churches of the Orthodox, adorned for the temples of God in every place in the world.

Listen to another true witness testifying to this holy fellowship of our father the saint John Kame: Isaiah the prophet also says that he saw in the beginning the glory of God, so he prophesied concerning what would be and said, "So let there be in the last time five cities in the land of Egypt speaking one language together."[11] Therefore, he gave us a symbol for these five holy monasteries, which God confirmed in the mountain of Scetis, according

---

10 Arabic, *haikal*. Literally: temple.
11 Cf. Isaiah 19:18.

to His holy will, and said, "Let them speak one language." And what is this one language, except the upright Orthodox faith, that which was preached in the holy monasteries. So we confessed a Holy Trinity in oneness, and oneness in Trinity, equal without separation and alteration, as our saintly fathers, the teachers of the Church, commanded us.

The History of the Life of Abba John Kame

Behold, my beloved, I have put your hearts at rest by proving the holy fellowship from the Lord's words, which He made with his servant through the angel who appeared to him in the beginning and proclaimed to him of that which would be. And he fulfilled the covenant which St. Mary made with him. And perhaps one of the unbelievers may say with envy, "How dare you proclaim to us that which the early fathers wrote to us beforehand." But listen to me, so that I may put your hearts at rest, and know that the words that I say are not lies but the truth, because trustworthy elders related to us the Life of our blessed father. For they had written it beforehand through his disciple Father Shenouti, he who knew all his virtues, and he is true in all his testimonies.

But the Life of our blessed father was preserved in the hearts of the brethren, the elders reading it [for] preservation and preaching to those coming after them, until it reached us. And they gave testimony

The Life of Abba John Kame

to us, for the sake of our righteous father, and we received the words of their preaching, because we know that their testimony is true.

We have written to you a part of his Life, to remind you of a few of his virtues.

Our father the saint Abba John Kame is pleased with us, by the greatness of his blessed remembrance, and although he lacks nothing of the virtues because of the perfection of his life, some of them remained hidden, when they washed it,[12] until the time of my poverty. For we found it written in old books like the law of the Lord when it was hidden in the days of Joram King of Israel, to the time of Josiah; and the Passover of the Lord was not proclaimed since the days of the judges to that time when Hilkiah the priest and Shaphan the scribe found the Book of the Law. So they told Josiah the king, and he believed in the God of Israel, and they held the Passover once again.

It is also written in the Book of the Law of the Lord that they burned it in the time wherein the Chaldeans destroyed Jerusalem, and after a long time Ezra the scribe explained it,[13] and he wrote it once more according as the Holy Spirit came upon him again.

---

12   It seems that someone tried to destroy the manuscript by putting it in water.
13   Here ends the missing part from the Coptic Life, which was translated from the Arabic Life.

Now these things I have said concerning them that deny with unconvinced opinion, believing not those things which we tell of the life of our father Abba John Kame. But woe to such as these, for they shall perish in their denial, even as Korah; they shall be under the curse of Balaam. Isaiah the prophet tells of their shame, saying, "Woe unto them that say of truth that it is falsehood, woe unto them that say of the light that it is darkness, woe unto them that say of that which is sweet that it is bitter." Our Savior says, "If one caused to stumble one of these little ones that believe on me, it would be good for him that a mill-stone were hanged about his body and that he were drowned in the sea;" and, "Woe to that man through whom the occasion of stumbling comes." Hear again, O you that deny, that I may convince your heart through the holy Scriptures. For seeing that the lawless Jews hid the holy Cross and the tomb of Christ and spoke falsehood concerning His resurrection, after 300 years Cyriacus revealed it by command of the King Constantine (and) heaven and earth were filled with its holy glory. Now these things I relate, O my beloved, that you may believe. For by the will of God, we have written unto you a small portion from the Life of our blessed father. Seeing therefore that they that believe have power for all things, yet have not the unbelievers a single penny. But why do I say these things and others also? Who can hinder the winds of heaven, or who can hide the rays of the sun, or who can hide the light of the moon? Neither can a city be hid that is set upon a hill, according to the saying of the Lord; and by this we believe that no adversary has power to hide the Life of our holy father Abba John Kame, of whom God-clad men, worthy of trust, with one accord bore witness. And we too have proclaimed it, to the glory of the name of God, as a remembrance for ever of our holy father, a boast also to us, his children, knowing surely that there is nothing hid that shall not be known. For this cause we have begun to speak thus far. Verily, O my beloved, we are gladdened today in the commemoration of our holy father, like them that are gladdened with wine. If there was joy for the people of the children of Israel when the ark returned unto them from out the land of the gentiles, then how great indeed is our joy in the discovery of the Life of our holy father! If the ark struck the gentiles and Dagon their god, even so did the name of the Life of our father strike Satan and his wicked demons. If the Lord blessed the house of Aminadab by the bringing in of the ark unto his house, even so shall the Lord bless everyone who shall write the book of the Life of our father and bring it in unto his house in faith, and him that shall hear it. Seeing that we have said sufficient unto your benevolence, O my beloved, you God-loving people, bearing witness unto you with faithful proofs, that by the will of God he revealed unto us the Life of our God-clad father at this present time, that it might be for a comfort unto us. God has not left it hidden under the bushel, but rather has set it upon the golden candle-stick and its rays of light have reached unto the uttermost ends of all the earth.

The Attempt to Plunder the Monastery

Hear further and I shall tell you of this other wonder whereof we are told, that was done after the death of our holy father. It happened in the time of the great famine that was in the 682nd year of the Holy Martyrs [AD 966], that there was great affliction over all the land because of the hunger that prevailed. And some treacherous men gathered together and made a band, that they should break into the community of our holy father and despoil it. And having taken ladders, they set them up against the wall, that they might descend and slay the old men and despoil the sanctuary. O, the great wonder that then happened! Suddenly there appeared great black serpents, fearful in their form, and rushed upon them, wishing to devour them. And immediately they were afraid and came down quickly from there, and they went to many other places of the wall and they saw the serpents pursuing after them. Immediately they knew that it was a power of God that watched over them and they departed in fear. And when they arose in the morning they came to the monastery and told the brethren those things they had attempted to do and those that they had seen; and they established peace with them for ever. And the brethren, when they heard these things, gave thanks to God, who had saved them from this bitter death. This gift was theirs through the mediation of the holy Mother of God, Mary, to the glory of the name of our holy father, because of the covenant that she had established with him, saying, "I will be with your children and will save them for your sake unto the end;" and this she fulfilled unto him in deed and in word of truth. And many among them bear witness unto us that she appeared unto them face to face and told them great mysteries, but especially our father Shenouti, he that was a successor to our blessed father and became ruler over the community.

Concluding Remarks

Let us content ourselves thus far, lest the discourse increase greatly; for we have left out much on account of those without faith. Verily my whole time and the remainder of my years shall not suffice me, that I may tell a small portion of your glory, O my lord father, nor can my mind nor my tongue tell of your honor, O beloved of Christ, O you well-famed of the Holy Spirit. You were the friend of God, even as Abraham; you did offer your body as a sacrifice unto Him, even as Isaac; you were wise as Joseph, the Lord gave you a lot like unto Ephraim and Manasseh; you did behold the glory of God, even as Moses; you did make laws for your people like unto him;

the Lord entrusted you with the priesthood, even as Aaron; you did pray for your people like unto Phinehas; the word of the Lord came unto you, even as Jeremiah the prophet; you were filled with the Holy Spirit, like unto the apostles; you did trample on all the power of the enemy, you did trample on all his desires, you did scatter all his counsels; you did bring low the violence of desire and all the wiles of his passions which take many forms and with which he has deceived many, through fornication that contends with the flesh. But you, O our father, you did make your members a temple of the Holy Spirit, because of your purity. For you did purify your five senses and were faithful with that which is yours. You did take the five talents and traded with them, and they made five talents, and your pound made ten pounds. You did give them unto your Lord with gladness and he honored you in the midst of your fellows and granted you ten exalted grades, filled with glory in heaven. You did flourish as the palm-tree, you did grow broad as the cedars of Lebanon; your perfume has spread abroad as a lily from the purity of your virginity. You did become a ruler to those of the desert and a captain of monks; you did become a fountain of righteousness and a lawgiver of virtue. You were a haven of salvation for many souls, you became a sage and a teacher and a leader for many peoples; you were an Israelite in whom is no guile; you did become a sweet savor, acceptable before God and his angels. Unto whom shall I liken you, with what shall I honor you, O our holy father? Verily you are likened to a golden bell; when it sounds the people rejoice. Verily you were a light, shining forth greatly in heaven and upon the earth. You were a sweet-smelling rose in the churches of the orthodox and the elect doctors tell of your honor. Therefore I beseech you, O my lord father, receive of my hands my little gift, poor though it be; and do number me also with the widow, that cast in two mites into the treasury. For I am an unlearned and ignorant man and untried in speech, therefore have me in remembrance before our Lord Jesus Christ, that he may forgive me, even me the humblest one both my many sins and all my errors of tongue. And I beseech you, O God-loving people, gathered together in this holy place today, blame me not that I attempted a great matter, too high for my capacity in that I should tell a small portion from the Life of our father, Abba John Kame.

And the measure is reached that we should bring the discourse to an end. May it be unto us all that we attain unto a little compassionate mercy, through the mediation of the lady of us all, the holy Mary, and the mediation of the archangels Michael and Gabriel and Raphael and the entreaties of all the Saints that have pleased God and the holy prayers of our father that loves his children; through the grace and the compassion and the lovingkindness of our Lord, our God, and our Savior, Jesus Christ, through whom all glory, all honor and all worship befit the Father, with him and with the Holy Spirit, life-giving and consubstantial with Him, now and at all times and for all eternity, Amen.

Mercy to him that writes. Amen.

Peace to him that reads. Amen.

Understanding to him that hears. Amen.

APPENDIX A: THE HISTORY OF THE RELICS OF ABBA JOHN KAME

The report of the transfer of the relics of the saint Abba John Kame to the Monastery of our Lady the Virgin, [known as] of the Syrians, in Scetis[14]

On the 21st of [the month of] Hathor, 1232 of the Martyrs [AD 1515], the body of the great saint, Abba John Kame the priest was transferred from his monastery which was in the area[15] of the monasteries, at a distance of about three kilometers toward the south-east from the monastery of the saint Abba Pishoi. In it [that is, the area], there were the monastery of the great saint, Abba John

---

14 *Serat Anba Yahnis Kama wa Tareikh Dair Al-Souryan* [The Life of Abba John Kame and the History of the Monastery of the Syrians]. (Wadi Al-Natrun, Egypt: The Monastery of our Lady the Virgin of the Syrians, 2007), 51–51. This report was found in a margin in the manuscript of the Synaxarion (number 6\221) in the library of the Monastery of Baramous.

15 Literally: pond or pool.

the Short, which was their largest; the monastery of the great saint, Abba John Kame the priest; the monastery of the Ethiopians; the monastery of the Armenians; and the cemetery of the fathers, the monks.

These monasteries were ruined in the end of the fifteenth century and the early sixteenth century, because of the drastic decline in the number of their monks, and [because of] the attack of white ants on their wood, and also because of the inability of the very few monks, who were left and were extremely poor, to renovate them. The ruins of these monasteries still exist and are visible until now.

The remaining monks of the monastery of Abba John Kame came to the monastery of our Lady the Virgin (of the Syrians), carrying with them the relics of their father Abba John Kame in a wooden cylinder, and placed it in a relics cabinet in the monastery. And [they brought] with them a marble stone, on which is recorded, in the Coptic language, the date of the departure of the saint, the 25th of Koiahk 575 of the Martyrs [AD 859], and they fixed it in the wall of the first chorus in the church of our Lady the Virgin of the Syrians, which is still present until now.

The blessing of this great saint be with us all, and to our Lord be the glory always, forever. Amen.

APPENDIX B: THE MONASTERY OF ABBA TEROTI

The Monastery of Abba Teroti,[16] the teacher of St. Abba John Kame[17]

In the days of this father, the teacher of St. John Kame, the Monastery of St. Macarius the Great was flourishing and populated with monks. It was like a great university and a city for governing. The number of monks grew, to the extent that the Monastery of St. Macarius had no place for them to live in; therefore, it became necessary that small monasteries be established, only affiliated with the Monasteries of St. Macarius the Great and St. John the Short. They were called *lavra* [Gr. λαύρα], a Greek word meaning a small courtyard or a group

---

16   Arabic: Derodi.

17   *Al-Kidees Anba Yahnis Kama: Al-Qis Al-Batoul* [The Saint Abba John Kame, the Celibate Priest], Deacon Youssef Habib, ed. (Egypt, 1971), 30–32. The content of this book was taken from manuscripts from the Monastery of Baramous.

of dispersed cells. It was used for monastic groups in Egypt, Palestine, and Syria, under the management of an elder[18], such as the Monastery of Abba Zacharias and the Monastery of Saints Abraam and George.

These small monasteries are also called the Great Cell, and in Coptic *ti nishti enri* [Cop. ϯⲛⲓϣϯ ⲛ̀ⲣⲓ], and some had their own church and cells. And they were attributed either to the country of the monks of the cells or to an excellent monk among the brethren. For example, the first type included the "Cell of the Damanhurians," that is the monastery designated for the monks from Damanhur; and the Cell of Batanoun for the monks from Batanoun, as it was mentioned in a manuscript in the Patriarchal Library in 991 of the Martyrs [AD 1275]. And of the second kind, there was the Cell of Philotheos, the Cell of Abraam and George, and the Cell of Teroti, the teacher of St. John Kame, from which came out the Patriarch Abba Gabriel.

There were about forty Great Cells. These Great Cells seem to have been built in the seventh century, when the number of the monks greatly increased, and through the passage of time they vanished.

In the fifteenth century, these small monasteries, which were affiliated with the Monastery of St. Macarius, began to vanish, as it was made clear from the history of the Patriarch Mattheos I, where the

---

18   Literally: a chief or ruler.

Lord worked a miracle on the night of his repose. The monks of the Monastery of St. Macarius related that they heard a movement and sound [coming] from the coffins of the Patriarchs, which called to them, saying, "Rise, go out, and open the gate, because our Father Mattheos is here, standing and knocking on the door." And they were inside the walls of the monastery, because the outer cells [the small monasteries] had been abandoned, and they opened [the gate] but found no one, so they marveled.

It seems that the most important factors that led to the disappearance of many of the cells and lofty monasteries in the fifteenth century are the epidemic that took place in the middle of the fourteenth century, and the famine that happened in AD 1474, and the plague which came in its wake.

ABOUT THE TEXT

This book contains the text of the Life of Abba John Kame, retrieved from the translation of the Coptic Life (Cod. Vat. Copt. LX) by M.H. Davis. This text was revised, and archaic words and phrases were replaced with their equivalent modern English counterparts. The Coptic Life is incomplete, however, because the manuscript translated by M.H. Davis is missing eight folios. We supplemented the missing part from the Arabic Life, which is complete and was published by the Monastery of the Syrians; therefore, the missing section was translated into English from Arabic, and was included in this present publication.

We also translated and included here the history of how the relics of Abba John were relocated from his monastery to the Monastery of the Syrians.

BIBLIOGRAPHY

Al-Kidees Anba Yahnis Kama: Al-Qis Al-Batoul [The Saint Abba John Kame, the Celibate Priest], Deacon Youssef Habib, ed. (Egypt, 1971). [Arabic]

Patrologia Orientalis 14, R. Griffin and F. Nau, eds. (Paris, France: Firmin-Didot, 1920), 322–370.

Serat Anba Yahnis Kama wa Tareikh Dair Al-Souryan [The Life of Abba John Kame and the History of the Monastery of the Syrians]. (Wadi Al-Natrun, Egypt: The Monastery of our Lady the Virgin of the Syrians, 2007). [Arabic]

www.ingramcontent.com/pod-product-compliance
Lightning Source LLC
Chambersburg PA
CBHW031433040426
42444CB00006B/796